Winds of *praise*

12 Worship Arrangements for One or More Wind Players
Arranged by Stan Pethel

PUBLICATIONS AVAILABLE:

SB1040 Piano / Score

SB1041 Flute / Oboe / Violin (with CD)

SB1042 Trumpet / Clarinet (with CD)

SB1043 French Horn (with CD)

SB1044 Trombone / Tuba / Cello (with CD)

SB1047 Alto Saxophone (with CD)

Shawnee Press

Exclusively Distributed By

Hal•Leonard® Corporation
7777 W. Bluemound Rd. P.O. Box 13819 Milwaukee, WI 53213

Visit Shawnee Press Online at www.shawneepress.com/songbooks

PREFACE

Winds of Praise was designed to allow for maximum flexibility of use. The uses range from full ensemble to solo instrument and piano. All of the arrangements will also work without piano. Just start at the first double bar or the pickups to the first double bar.

Here are some options:

1. Solo instrument and piano or track. The piano/score book works as accompaniment for all instruments as does the accompaniment CD.

2. Multiple instruments and piano or track. Just have one instrument play the solo part and the other(s) the ensemble part along with the piano or accompaniment CD. Use more players on the solo part if needed to project the melody.

3. For instruments only, with no piano or CD accompaniment, these combinations will work:

   a. Brass Quartet – trumpet 1 & 2 with trombone 1 & 2 parts will stand alone. Start at the first double bar.

   b. Brass Quintet or Brass Sextet – For quintet use trumpet 1 & 2, horn, trombone 1, and tuba. For sextet add trombone 2. Start at the double bar.

   c. Other ensemble combinations. As long as trumpet 1 & 2 and trombone 1 & 2 are covered, the other parts will only add to the fullness of the ensemble. Piano adds even more and fills out the harmony. For instruments only start at the double bar, with piano starting at the beginning.

   d. Remember these instrumental substitutions. Violins and oboes can play or double the flute part. Clarinets can play or double the trumpet parts. Cellos, bassoons, and baritones can play the trombone part. Bass trombone players may want to try the tuba part as well. The tuba part can also be covered by a bass setting from an electric keyboard to add depth to the sound.

These arrangements are good lengths for preludes, offertories, and featured instrumental performance in both church services and church or school concerts. The level of difficulty ranges from 2 ½ to 3. Most are also in good vocal range should you choose to add choral or congregational singing at appropriate places. If you have a rhythm section of piano, guitar, bass, and drums, there are chord symbols provided with some basic drum suggestions in the piano score.

Best wishes with these arrangements in your area of musical ministry. Let us know at Shawnee Press if you find them useful, and what else we can do to assist with your instrumental needs.

Stan Pethel

CONTENTS

Come, Now Is the Time to Worship

Trombone 1&2
(Cello, Bassoon, Bass clef Baritone)
Ensemble

Music by **BRIAN DOERKSEN**
Arranged by **STAN PETHEL**

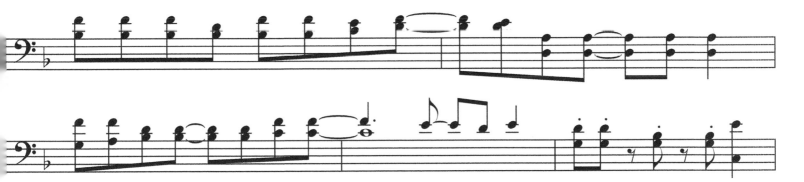

Come, Now Is the Time to Worship

Trombone
(Cello, Bassoon, Bass Clef Baritone)
Solo

Music by **BRIAN DOERKSEN**
Arranged by **STAN PETHEL**

Come, Now Is the Time to Worship

Tuba
(Arco bass 8va)
Ensemble

Music by **BRIAN DOERKSEN**
Arranged by **STAN PETHEL**

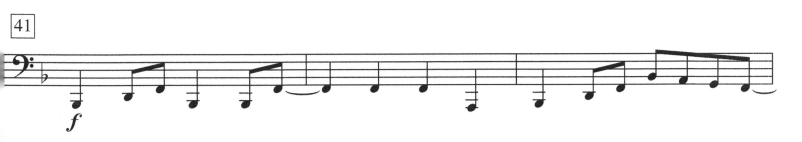

He Is Exalted

Trombone 1&2
(Cello, Bassoon, Baritone Bass Clef)
Ensemble

Music by **TWILA PARIS**
Arranged by **STAN PETHEL**

With motion (♩. = *ca. 72*)

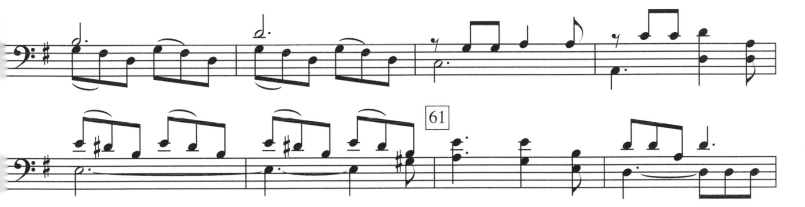

He Is Exalted

Trombone
(Cello, Bassoon, Bass Clef Baritone)
Solo

Music by **TWILA PARIS**
Arranged by **STAN PETHEL**

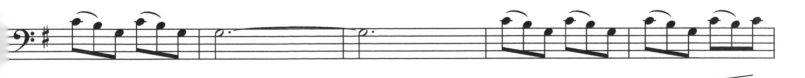

He Is Exalted

14

Tuba
(Double Bass 8va)
Ensemble

Music by **TWILA PARIS**
Arranged by **STAN PETHEL**

15

Here I Am to Worship

Trombone 1&2
(Cello, Bassoon, Baritone Bass Clef)
Ensemble

Music by **TIM HUGHES**
Arranged by **STAN PETHEL**

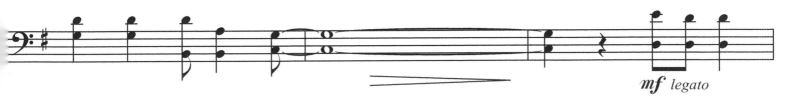

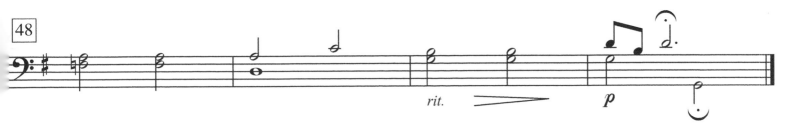

Here I Am to Worship

Trombone
(Bassoon, Baritone Bass Clef, Cello)
Solo

Music by **TIM HUGHES**
Arranged by **STAN PETHEL**

Tuba
(Arco Bass 8 va)
Ensemble

Here I Am to Worship

Music by **TIM HUGHES**
Arranged by **STAN PETHEL**

In Christ Alone

Trombone 1&2
(Cello, Bassoon, Baritone Bass Clef)
Ensemble

Music by **KEITH GETTY** *and* **STUART TOWNEND**
Arranged by **STAN PETHEL**

Trombone
(Bassoon, Baritone Bass Clef,
Cello)
Solo

In Christ Alone

Music by **KEITH GETTY** and **STUART TOWNEND**
Arranged by **STAN PETHEL**

In Christ Alone

Tuba (Arco Bass 8 va)
Ensemble

Music by **KEITH GETTY** and **STUART TOWNEND**
Arranged by **STAN PETHEL**

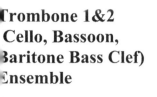

Trombone 1&2
(Cello, Bassoon,
Baritone Bass Clef)
Ensemble

Sanctuary

Music by **JOHN W. THOMPSON**
and **RANDY SCRUGGS**
Arranged by **STAN PETHEL**

Sanctuary

Trombone
(Bassoon, Baritone Bass Clef, Cello)
Solo

Music by **JOHN W. THOMPSON**
and **RANDY SCRUGGS**
Arranged by **STAN PETHEL**

Tuba
(Arco Bass 8 va)
Ensemble

Sanctuary

Music by **JOHN W. THOMPSON**
and **RANDY SCRUGGS**
Arranged by **STAN PETHEL**

How Great Is Our God

Trombone 1&2
(Cello, Bassoon, Baritone Bass Clef)
Ensemble

Music by **Chris Tomlin, Jesse Reeves,** *and* **Ed Cash**
Arranged by **STAN PETHEL**

How Great Is Our God

Tuba
(Arco Bass 8 va)
Ensemble

Music by **Chris Tomlin, Jesse Reeves,** *and* **Ed Cash**
Arranged by **STAN PETHEL**

How Great Is Our God

Trombone
(Bassoon, Baritone Bass Clef, Cello)
Solo

Music by **Chris Tomlin**, **Jesse Reeves**, *and* **Ed Cash**
Arranged by **STAN PETHEL**

Trombone 1&2
(Cello, Bassoon, Baritone
Bass Clef)
Ensemble

As the Deer

Music by **MARTIN NYSTROM**
Arranged by **STAN PETHEL**

As the Deer

Trombone
(Bassoon, Baritone Bass Clef, Cello)
Solo

Music by **MARTIN NYSTROM**
Arranged by **STAN PETHEL**

Tuba
(Arco Bass 8va)
Ensemble

As the Deer

Music by **MARTIN NYSTROM**
Arranged by **STAN PETHEL**

Lord, I Lift Your Name on High

Trombone 1&2
(Cello, Bassoon, Baritone Bass Clef)
Ensemble

Music by **RICK POUNDS**
Arranged by **STAN PETHEL**

Lord, I Lift Your Name on High

Trombone
(Bassoon, Baritone, Bass Clef, Cello)
Solo

Music by **RICK POUNDS**
Arranged by **STAN PETHEL**

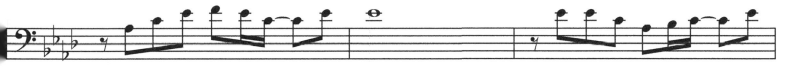

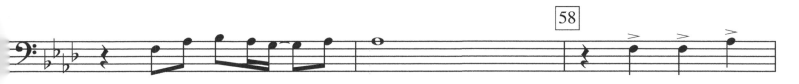

Lord, I Lift Your Name on High

Tuba
(Arco Bass 8va)
Ensemble

Music by **RICK POUNDS**
Arranged by **STAN PETHEL**

Above All

Trombone 1&2
(Cello, Bassoon, Baritone Bass Clef)
Ensemble

Music by **LENNY LEBRANC** *and* **PAUL BALOCHE**
Arranged by **STAN PETHEL**

Trombone
Bassoon, Baritone
(Bass Clef, Cello)
Solo

Above All

Music by **LENNY LEBRANC** *and* **PAUL BALOCHE**
Arranged by **STAN PETHEL**

Above All

Tuba
(Arco Bass 8va)
Ensemble

Music by **LENNY LEBRANC** *and* **PAUL BALOCHE**
Arranged by **STAN PETHEL**

Trombone 1&2
(Cello, Bassoon,
Baritone Bass Clef)
Ensemble

Jesus, Draw Me Close

Music by **RICK FOUNDS**
Arranged by **STAN PETHEL**

Jesus, Draw Me Close

Trombone
(Bassoon, Baritone Bass Clef, Cello)
Solo

Music by **RICK FOUNDS**
Arranged by **STAN PETHEL**

Tuba
(Arco Bass 8 va)
Ensemble

Jesus, Draw Me Close

Music by **RICK FOUNDS**
Arranged by **STAN PETHEL**

You Are My All In All

Trombone
(Bassoon, Baritone Bass Clef, Cello)
Solo

Music by **DENNIS JERNIGAN**
Arranged by **STAN PETHEL**

With an underlying beat (♩ = *ca. 72*)

You Are My All In All

Trombone 1&2
(Cello, Bassoon, Baritone Bass Clef)
Ensemble

Music by **DENNIS JERNIGAN**
Arranged by **STAN PETHEL**

With an underlying beat (♩ = *ca. 72*)

Tuba
(Arco Bass 8 va)
Ensemble

You Are My All In All

Music by **DENNIS JERNIGAN**
Arranged by **STAN PETHEL**

49

Shine, Jesus, Shine

Trombone 1&2
(Cello, Bassoon, Baritone Bass Clef)
Ensemble

Music by **GRAHAM KENDRICK**
Arranged by **STAN PETHEL**

mf *smoothly*

(Opt. Brass out to bar 48)

36

48 *Brass in - accented*

56

63

rit.

Shine, Jesus, Shine

Trombone
(Bassoon, Baritone Bass Clef, Cello)
Solo

Music by **GRAHAM KENDRICK**
Arranged by **STAN PETHEL**

Shine, Jesus, Shine

Tuba
(Arco Bass 8 va)
Ensemble

Music by **GRAHAM KENDRICK**
Arranged by **STAN PETHEL**